STEPHEN HAWKING

STEPHEN HAWKING

CELEBRATED PHYSICIST

MATT DOEDEN

LERNER PUBLICATIONS ◆ MINNEAPOLIS

Lerner Publications Company
An imprint of Lerner Publishing Group, Inc.
241 First Avenue North
Minneapolis, MN 55401 USA

For reading levels and more information, look up this title at www.lernerbooks.com.

Image credits: Eleanor Bentall/Corbis/Getty Images, p. 2; Milbert Orlando Brown/The Boston Globe/Getty Images, p. 6; Andrea Danti/Shutterstock.com, p. 8; Karwai Tang/Getty Images, p. 9; Anna Moskvina/Shutterstock.com, p. 11; Bettmann/Getty Images, pp. 12, 20; S-F/Shutterstock.com, p. 13; Man vyi/Wikimedia Commons, p. 14; John Kropewnicki/Shutterstock.com, p. 15; FlashMovie/Shutterstock.com, p. 16; David Levenson/Getty Images, p. 17; RDImages/Epics/Getty Images, p. 18; BlueRingMedia/Shutterstock.com, p. 19; Andrii Vodolazhskyi/Shutterstock.com, p. 21; local_doctor/Shutterstock.com, p. 23; Bob Mahoney/The LIFE Images Collection/Getty Images, p. 24; NASA/GSFC, p. 25; Claudio Divizia/Shutterstock.com, p. 26; Jean-Regis Rouston/Roger Viollet/Getty Images, p. 28; Brian Randle/Mirrorpix/Getty Images, p. 29; Gilles Bassignac/Gamma-Rapho/Getty Images, pp. 31, 32; Michael Stephens/PA Images/Getty Images, p. 33; Red Huber/Orlando Sentinel/Tribune News Service/Getty Images, p. 34; CBS Photo Archive/Getty Images, p. 35; Ramesh Pathania/Mint/Hindustan Times/Getty Images, p. 36; Danny Martindale/FilmMagic/Getty Images, p. 37; andrey_l/Shutterstock.com, p. 38; Daniel Leal-Olivas/AFP/Getty Images, p. 40; Benny Marty/Shutterstock.com, p. 41.

Cover: Paul. E. Alers/NASA/Getty Images.

Main body text set in Rotis Serif Std 55 Regular.
Typeface provided by Adobe Systems.

Library of Congress Cataloging-in-Publication Data

Names: Doeden, Matt, author.
Title: Stephen Hawking : celebrated physicist / Matt Doeden.
Description: Minneapolis : Lerner Publications, [2021] | Series: Gateway biographies | Includes bibliographical references and index. | Audience: Ages 9–14 | Audience: Grades 4–6 | Summary: "Readers learn about one of the most celebrated and inspiring physicists of all time, delving into Hawking's life story, cosmological discoveries, and disability activism"– Provided by publisher.
Identifiers: LCCN 2019055015 (print) | LCCN 2019055016 (ebook) | ISBN 9781541596733 (library binding) | ISBN 9781728413556 (paperback) | ISBN 9781728400341 (ebook)
Subjects: LCSH: Hawking, Stephen, 1942–2018–Juvenile literature. | Physicists–Great Britain–Biography–Juvenile literature. | Amyotrophic lateral sclerosis–Patients–Great Britain–Biography–Juvenile literature.
Classification: LCC QC16.H33 D64 2021 (print) | LCC QC16.H33 (ebook) | DDC 530.092 [B]–dc23

LC record available at https://lccn.loc.gov/2019055015
LC ebook record available at https://lccn.loc.gov/2019055016

Manufactured in the United States of America
1-47781-48218-3/2/2020

CONTENTS

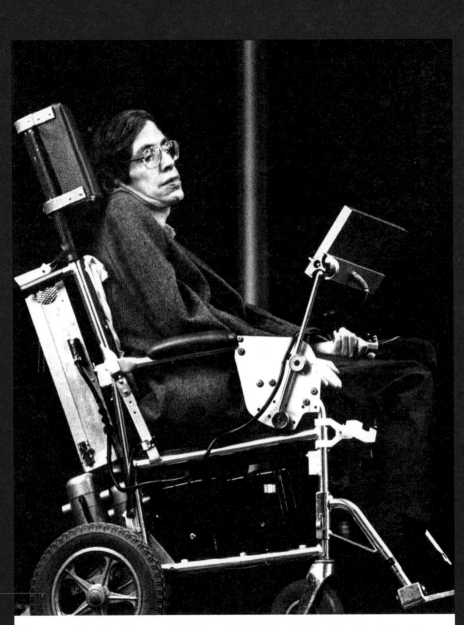

Recognized for his achievements in theoretical physics, Stephen Hawking lectured at universities around the world. This photo was taken at a lecture he gave at Northeastern University in Boston in 1990.

In 1974 Stephen Hawking sat in his wheelchair in his office. His mind was sharper than ever. He was a cosmologist, a scientist who studied the universe in all of its vastness. He centered his career on the study of black holes, objects so massive and dense that even light cannot escape their gravity. Yet in 1974 Hawking was thinking about the universe at its tiniest scale—the quantum universe, which operates at scales smaller than the atom. What he was about to discover would propel him into scientific fame.

Hawking understood the strangeness of quantum mechanics, where particles can pop in and out of existence and even exist in two places at the same time. He wondered how that quantum strangeness might affect a black hole. At the time, scientists thought of black holes as huge cosmic vacuum cleaners that sucked up mass and energy. Because of the black holes' intense gravity, that

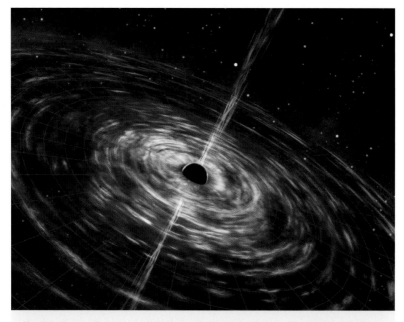
Hawking's most famous work in theoretical physics has to do with black holes.

mass and energy was gone forever, essentially removed from the rest of the universe. Hawking believed that black holes could only get bigger—never smaller.

The workings of quantum mechanics inspired him to dive deep into the mathematics of both the very large and the very tiny. After a lot of thinking and writing, he came to a conclusion that shocked the scientific world: black holes were not eternal. Physicists previously thought that black holes would last forever, because nothing could escape them. But Hawking found that quantum mechanics caused black holes to very slowly radiate, or leak, tiny amounts of energy. Over incredibly long spans of time, black holes would slowly evaporate, getting smaller and smaller, until they would explode with a force unlike any other in the universe. Hawking wrote about this discovery in a 1974 letter that was published in *Nature*.

At first, Hawking's theory was controversial. Many cosmologists didn't believe it. But over time, most found that Hawking's mathematics proved that it must be true. Hawking radiation, as it came to be known, was one of Hawking's greatest discoveries, and helped to make him one of the most famous and pioneering physicists of his generation.

Hawking authored and coauthored more than two hundred publications, including fifteen books.

Creative and Curious

Stephen William Hawking was born on January 8, 1942, in Oxford, England. His birth was on the three hundredth anniversary of the death of Galileo Galilei, who is often called the father of modern physics. Hawking was born into a well-educated family of humble means. Both of his parents, Frank and Isobel Hawking, had studied at Oxford University. After Stephen's birth, the family quickly grew, welcoming Stephen's sisters, Philippa and Mary, and brother, Edward. Their father frequently traveled, and he was often away from home for months at a time, leaving most of the parenting to their mother.

Stephen was a creative child. He loved to play games. However, he quickly grew bored with his games. So he invented his own. His creativity did not extend to his schooling, however. His parents sent him to Byron House, a nontraditional school that allowed students a great deal of freedom in their own learning. It was the sort of environment where one might expect the developing mind of one of history's greatest thinkers to thrive, but young Stephen struggled with such a self-driven learning style. He didn't learn to read until he was eight years old, very late compared to his peers and even to his sister Philippa, who learned to read at the age of four.

In 1950 the family moved to St Albans. Stephen's family valued education, and as a teenager, Stephen bounced from school to school, searching for the right fit. He even spent time at St Albans High School for Girls, which did accept boys, despite its name. He eventually settled at St Albans

Hawking grew up in the English town of St Albans, which is well known for its historic cathedral.

School. His friends there remember him as a practical joker and as a kid who didn't get down on himself, even when he suffered at the hands of school bullies. He was an active, but not athletic, young man who was quick to make friends.

Stephen loved to build and tinker. He made model airplanes that rarely flew well. He dabbled in electronics, although he had limited electrical skills. Once, when trying to turn a television set into an amplifier, Stephen accidentally gave himself a powerful shock. Later, Stephen and his friends built their own crude computer—a rarity in the 1950s. The computer didn't work very well, but the

Although Hawking never met him, Albert Einstein (1879–1955) inspired Hawking's work in physics.

excitement it generated got Stephen what may have been his first bit of publicity, a story in the local newspaper.

Stephen was, he said, not a particularly outstanding student. "My classwork was very untidy," he later wrote, "and my handwriting was the despair of my teachers. But my classmates gave me the nickname Einstein, so presumably they saw signs of something better." Stephen's best subjects were math and science, possibly leading his friends to nickname him after famous physicist Albert Einstein.

As Stephen neared graduation, he planned to study at a university. His father wanted him to attend University College in Oxford to study medicine. Stephen partly agreed. At the age of seventeen, he enrolled at Oxford—not to study medicine but to study physics instead. His father protested, arguing that an education in physics offered few good career paths. But Stephen didn't want to be a doctor. He wanted to peer deeper into the mysteries of the universe.

Oxford University was established as early as 1096, making it the second-oldest university still in operation in the world. The oldest is the University of Bologna in Italy.

University Life

Early on, Hawking was unimpressed with university life. He struggled to fit in and found little challenge in his studies. He called the physics program, "ridiculously easy. You could get through without going to any lectures . . . you didn't have to remember many facts, just a few equations."

Eventually, Hawking made friends and settled in at Oxford, and many began to notice his intelligence. His friend Derek Powney remembers how in one class, students were given a list of problems to solve. They

The Front Quad of University College at Oxford was built in the mid-seventeenth century and has changed very little in the centuries since.

According to one of Hawking's former rowing teammates, he was a very skilled coxswain but had little interest in becoming the best on the team.

had a week to figure out as many as they could. Most students solved one or two. Hawking didn't even start on the list until the morning it was due, yet he solved ten. "Even at Oxford, we must all have been remarkably stupid by his standards," Powney said.

During Hawking's second year at Oxford, he joined the school's rowing team. At first, it may have seemed like an odd fit. Hawking was slight of build and lacked the muscles and athleticism needed for rowing. But his body size made him perfect for one role, the coxswain. On a rowing team, the coxswain sits at the front of the boat and steers it with a rudder. So a person with a slight frame and little body weight is ideal. The smaller the coxswain, the less extra work the rowers need to do to push the boat through the water. Hawking's loud voice was also perfect for barking out commands to the rest of the team.

Hawking's time on the rowing team was one of the happiest of his life. He fell in with a popular crowd. He was exerting himself in ways that he never had before. For the first time in his life, he felt like an athlete. He had come a long way from the friendly, shy seventeen-year-old who had arrived at Oxford.

During his third and final year at Oxford, Hawking was faced with a difficult decision. What area of study would he focus on after earning his degree? He narrowed it down to two choices: cosmology and particle physics. Cosmologists study the universe and all of its massive

The standard cosmological model says that the universe started from a tiny point and expanded outward in a so-called big bang.

structures. Particle physicists study the tiniest bits of matter and the particles that make them up. It was a choice between the very large and the very small. Hawking chose cosmology. He was to begin his studies of the universe in 1962 at the University of Cambridge.

It was an exciting time in Hawking's life. His studies were about to take him in a new and fascinating direction. He was enjoying a vibrant social life, and he

Jane Hawking, formerly Jane Wilde, in 2007

had just found love with Jane Wilde, the sister of one of his friends. Yet a new concern had crept up in Hawking's mind. He noticed signs of a health problem. His life was about to change in a way he never expected.

Life Changes and a New Focus

In 1962, while still at Oxford, Hawking had begun to notice changes in his strength and movements. As he began studying at Cambridge, the symptoms grew more noticeable.

The University of Cambridge, where Hawking attended graduate school, is the second-oldest English language university in the world, after Oxford.

"In my third year at Oxford, I noticed that I seemed to be getting more clumsy," he recalled. "I fell over once or twice for no apparent reason. But it was not until I was at Cambridge that my father noticed, and took me to the family doctor. He referred me to a specialist, and shortly after my twenty-first birthday, I went into [the] hospital for tests."

Hawking endured a two-week battery of tests. Doctors took muscle samples from his arm, injected his spine with fluid that they could see on an X-ray, and did many more tests. As time dragged on, Hawking's dread grew worse and worse. It was becoming clear that the doctors thought something was seriously wrong. "After all [the tests], they didn't tell me what I had, except that it was not multiple sclerosis, and that I was an atypical case," Hawking said. "I gathered, however, that they expected it to continue to get worse, and that there was nothing they could do, except give me vitamins. I could see that they didn't expect them to have much effect. I didn't feel like asking for more details, because they were obviously bad."

The doctors diagnosed Hawking with amyotrophic lateral sclerosis (ALS). ALS is also called motor neuron disease (MND), or Lou Gehrig's disease. It was devastating news for Hawking and his family. ALS causes a person's motor neurons—the cells that carry signals to the muscles—to wither away. There was no cure. According to Hawking's doctors, ALS was a degenerative disease. That means it would never get better, only worse. Hawking, at just twenty-one years old, was told he had only two years to live.

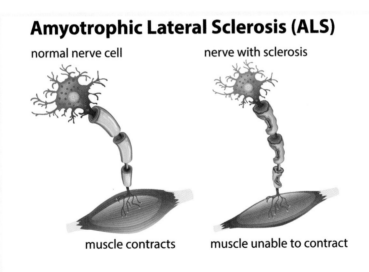

Amyotrophic Lateral Sclerosis (ALS)

normal nerve cell

nerve with sclerosis

muscle contracts

muscle unable to contract

This illustration shows the difference between a nerve cell unaffected (*left*) and affected (*right*) by ALS. The cell affected by ALS deteriorates over time and eventually dies.

LOU GEHRIG

Lou Gehrig was the heart of the New York Yankees baseball team through much of the 1920s and 1930s. The first baseman helped the Yankees win six World Series titles. He won two Most Valuable Player awards along the way. He earned the nickname Iron Horse for playing in a record 2,130 consecutive games.

But by 1939, Gehrig began to notice physical changes to his body. His power was gone. His coordination was growing worse. On his thirty-sixth birthday, he was diagnosed with ALS. Gehrig's ALS progressed quickly. He died less than two years after his diagnosis.

A portrait of Lou Gehrig in 1927. Major League Baseball honors his legacy by giving the Lou Gehrig Memorial Award to players who exhibit integrity and contribute to their community.

While the nerve cells controlling Hawking's muscles were affected by ALS, those in his brain were not, allowing him to continue pursuing his career in physics.

Hawking fell into a deep depression. For a time, he lost interest in his studies. But eventually, he accepted his diagnosis. According to Hawking, one night he dreamed that he was given the choice to sacrifice his own life to save others. In the dream, he chose to do so. The dream gave him focus and clarity. He was going to use whatever time he had left, even if it was just a few years, to achieve his goals and make a difference in the world. And he saw a bright side to his choice to be a theoretical physicist. It was one of few professions where his mind was the only tool he needed. Since ALS affected only the body, not the mind, he would continue his studies into the mysteries of the universe for as much time as he had left.

And so Hawking started to do the only thing he could. He dedicated himself to his studies as never before. In 1964, a year after his diagnosis, he asked Wilde to marry him. She agreed. They were married a year later. Much to Hawking's surprise, three years came and went, and he was still very much alive. His condition was progressing far slower than doctors had expected. By 1965 he needed to use a cane to get around. And he'd lost a great deal of his fine motor control, needed for actions such as writing. But on the whole, his health was remarkably good for someone with ALS.

Peering into Black Holes

Hawking's diagnosis gave him a focus unlike any he had ever had before. Although his ALS was progressing remarkably slowly, he always knew that his time could be cut short. Hawking dove deep into his study of cosmology at Cambridge. At the time, most cosmologists believed in one of two main models of the universe. One model was the steady state theory. It said that the universe was eternal and generally unchanging. The second was the big bang theory. It said that the universe had started out as a single point that rapidly expanded, or exploded, into a universe that continues to change and grow.

Hawking favored the big bang theory. He wondered if the physics inside a singularity—a point of infinite density and zero volume, or size, inside a black hole—could tell scientists about the physics of the early universe. He wrote his thesis, a long essay that is the focal point of a graduate student's work, on that idea. The paper earned him his PhD (doctoral degree). At the age of twenty-three, he was officially Dr. Stephen Hawking.

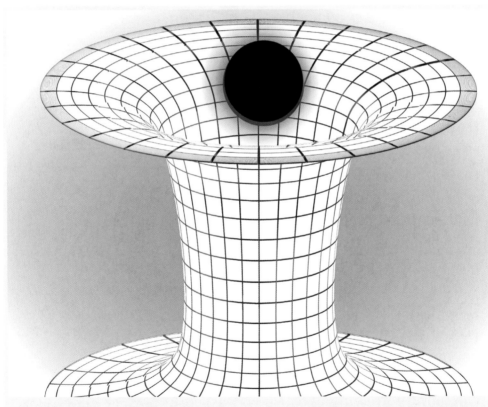

When black holes were first theorized to exist, some physicists thought they might be wormholes to other parts of the universe or other dimensions.

At the time, the idea of black holes was still fairly new to cosmology. The theories of gravity and general relativity suggested that when very large stars ran out of fuel to burn, they collapsed in on themselves and became black holes. But no one had produced any proof that such objects really existed, and many doubted they did. Even Albert Einstein had thought that black holes were far too strange to be anything more than a mathematical theory.

Hawking was good friends with fellow physicist Sir Roger Penrose (b. 1931), who is a pioneer in the fields of black holes and cosmology.

Hawking was convinced they were real, however. And he devoted much of his time to studying them and their behavior. He collaborated, or worked with, famous physicist Roger Penrose on a theory that the universe started out as a singularity. In time, scientific evidence showed that the steady state theory of the universe probably wasn't true, and most cosmologists accepted the big bang theory—with Hawking and Penrose's singularity model at its core. Hawking's status in the scientific community grew quickly. He was asked to present his findings at scientific conferences. But by then his disease had progressed and his speech was affected. Worried that his audience would have a hard time understanding him, Hawking had fellow scientists present his findings for him.

Hawking's professional life was taking off. So was his family life. Jane Hawking gave birth to their first child, Robert, in 1967. Lucy followed in 1969, and Timothy came ten years later. As Hawking's ALS progressed, he began using a wheelchair to get around. Jane focused on pursuing her PhD and parenting while Hawking worked on solving the mysteries of the universe.

In 1973 Hawking, along with mathematician and coauthor G. F. R. Ellis, published Hawking's first book, *The Large Scale Structure of Space-Time.* The book investigated the booming field of cosmology and described how scientists were coming to new conclusions

The word *space-time* refers to the concept that the three dimensions of space are connected to a fourth dimension, time, to create our universe. General relativity theorizes that disturbances in space-time cause gravity.

on subjects such as singularities, causality (or cause and effect), and the structure of space and time itself. A year later, Hawking presented his findings on the radiation of black holes, which became known as Hawking radiation.

Hawking was showered with honors, including the Albert Einstein Award, for his work. He was inducted into the Royal Society, a fellowship of scientists, in 1974. At the age of thirty-two, he was one of the youngest scientists ever accepted into the society. Five years later, Hawking was appointed Lucasian Professor of Mathematics at Cambridge. Hawking was becoming one of the most powerful thinkers in physics.

The Royal Society, headquartered in London, England, is the oldest national scientific institution in the world.

A BETTING MAN

Hawking became famous for making bets with other scientists. One of his first bets came in 1974. Scientists had discovered a distant X-ray signal called Cygnus X-1. Physicist Kip Thorne bet that it was a black hole. Hawking bet that it wasn't. Sixteen years later, Hawking admitted that Thorne was right. He paid off the bet, buying Thorne a magazine subscription. Hawking's wagers became the stuff of legends in scientific circles. He often bet against his own theories so that he'd be happy when he finally had to pay them off.

Struggles and Triumphs

Even as Hawking's career was taking off, his health was declining. The Hawking family lived in a two-story home, and Hawking's bedroom was on the second floor. It was a nightly struggle for him to get up the stairs, and he refused help. Some close to him called it toughness. Others described it as pure stubbornness. Hawking understood that the day would come when he would not be able to perform the task at all, and he was determined to be self-reliant for as long as he possibly could.

By the 1980s, Hawking relied on nurses, family, and graduate students for basic care, including feeding, washing, and dressing. He communicated mainly through interpreters. Meanwhile, Hawking's relationship with Jane Hawking grew more distant, and the pair began to drift apart.

But Hawking's mind was intact, and he wanted to delve into one of the greatest mysteries of science: Where did the universe come from? The big bang theory was widely accepted by this time, but physicists still struggled to explain how the universe came into being. What had caused the big bang? Had time and space existed before it? Hawking worked with fellow physicist Jim Hartle to propose one explanation: the Hawking-Hartle state. They believed that before the big bang, time itself did not exist. Hawking also worked to explain the conditions of the very early universe, including cosmological inflation, the idea that the young universe expanded at an incredibly rapid rate.

By 1982 Hawking was an accomplished author. But most of his writing had been directed at fellow scientists. Hawking wanted to reach out to a much broader audience. He wanted to share the strangeness and wonder that he saw in the universe with people who lacked a scientific

As Hawking lost his ability to write, he had to learn how to express his ideas in new ways. He began to visualize mathematical equations using geometric shapes. A fellow physicist compared him to Mozart.

Although he was hesitant to begin using a wheelchair at first, Hawking later became known for driving his wheelchair at high speeds and joking about running over people's feet.

background. It was a tall task. Hawking was used to communicating in very technical terms. For this project, he would have to adopt a completely new way of writing and explaining ideas. His declining health was another stumbling block, as it slowed down his writing. Yet Hawking charged ahead with the project.

In the summer of 1985, it looked as if Hawking might never get the chance to finish what he had started. He traveled to Switzerland to discuss quantum theory with fellow physicists. While there, he fell ill with pneumonia and slipped into a coma. His prognosis was grim. Doctors did not believe he would survive. Jane Hawking rushed to Switzerland to be by his side.

"The doctors thought I was so far gone that they offered Jane [the option] to turn off the machine," Hawking explained. Yet Hawking was no stranger to defying the medical odds, and he pulled out of the coma. "The weeks of intensive care that followed were the darkest of my life. But slowly the drugs worked, though a small incision in my throat robbed me of my ability to talk. I was then put on a ventilator and hopes of finishing my book seemed over."

The loss of his ability to speak was a devastating blow for Hawking. He was left with only a crude form of communication, indicating words and letters on a card by raising an eyebrow to convey simple messages. Discussing advanced scientific theories and writing books were out of the question.

Then came a ray of hope. Words Plus was developing a computer program that allowed a user to select words and commands with a hand clicker. Another piece of software then turned the words into sound. When the company learned of Hawking's condition, it donated a system to him. The early version of the program was still rough. But it gave Hawking the ability to speak at a rate of about fifteen words per minute. It wasn't much, but it was enough. Hawking got back to work.

Beginnings and Endings

In 1988 Hawking finally published his book, *A Brief History of Time*. The book covers a wide range of scientific ideas, but focuses mainly on the big bang, general relativity, and quantum mechanics. Hawking didn't know how people would receive the book. His goal,

Jane Hawking (*left*) assists Stephen Hawking with his computer at an event in France. Copies of the French edition of *A Brief History of Time* sit on the table in front of them.

he said, was to write something that almost anyone could read and understand. But publishers had cautioned him that the book wouldn't have the mass appeal he imagined.

They were wrong. Hawking's two-hundred-page book was an overnight sensation. Critics loved it. According to the *New York Times*, "[Hawking's] book is a rare sharing of confidence by a scientist with uncommon courage, a dazzling vision, and an impish sense of humor."

The first print run of *A Brief History of Time* sold out in just a few days. It spent a stunning 147 weeks on the

Stephen Hawking with Jane in 1989

New York Times best-seller list. The book sold more than ten million copies, cementing Hawking's status as an international celebrity.

But even as Hawking's career was soaring to new heights, his family life was falling apart. His marriage had been strained for years. Hawking's fame, along with the care Jane needed to provide for him as well as the children, had been difficult for her. Over time, Hawking had become an outspoken atheist. His view that God did not exist clashed with her religious upbringing and beliefs. The issues were more than the marriage could handle. The couple separated around 1990 and finally divorced in 1995. Not long after, Hawking married Elaine Mason, one of his nurses. This second marriage ended eleven years later, in 2007.

Through it all, Hawking never stopped asking questions about the nature of the universe. He became focused on his idea of cosmic inflation shortly after the big bang. Hawking was convinced that the universe had not just had one beginning but many. Hawking called this idea top-down cosmology. Instead of tracing the history of the universe from the past to the present, he did the opposite. He believed that early conditions of the universe depended on the observed conditions of the present, an argument that actually suggested that events of the present can affect conditions in the past.

During the 1990s, however, much of Hawking's attention was on bringing science to the masses. In

Hawking and his second wife, Elaine Mason, after their wedding ceremony

Hawking expressed a desire to travel to space. In 2007 he went on a zero-gravity flight to experience weightlessness, which was the closest he would get to space.

1997 he starred in a six-part television series called *Stephen Hawking's Universe* that aired on PBS. In 2001 he published *The Universe in a Nutshell*, a sort of sequel to *A Brief History of Time*. In the new book, Hawking focused on the search for a theory that combines quantum mechanics, the physics of the very small, with general relativity, the physics of the very large. Physicists, including Hawking, have searched for this unification theory, also called the theory of everything, for decades with little success. The new book sold fairly well but never approached the popularity or acclaim Hawking had received for *A Brief History of Time*.

A Voice for Science

Many physicists believe that by the twenty-first century, most of Hawking's scientific achievement was behind him. His status as a pop culture icon had made him a strong voice for science, but he also continued to take part in scientific debates. One of the most famous of them revolved around what happened to matter, energy, and the information they contain when they fall into a black hole. Hawking had long believed that the quantum information in this mass and energy is lost to the universe forever.

TAKING THE STAGE

In 1993 Hawking made a guest appearance on the TV show, *Star Trek: The Next Generation.* Hawking played himself, virtually generated by a computer, playing poker with several of the show's major characters. It was the first of several television roles that would help fuel Hawking's celebrity status. He later added recurring roles as himself on shows such as *The Simpsons, Futurama,* and *The Big Bang Theory.* He even appeared in the 2017 video game *Futurama: Worlds of Tomorrow.*

Hawking as he appeared on *Star Trek*

Lucy Hawking (b. 1969), in addition to being a published author and science educator, is an advocate for people with disabilities.

The black hole served as a quantum eraser, in his view. However, most physicists argued that quantum information could never be lost. It must be preserved, somehow. In 2004 Hawking famously admitted that he had been wrong. He later called the belief the biggest blunder of his career.

Science remained a focus of Hawking's life, but he also turned his attention to other matters. He became an active voice for several causes. He fought for more rights for the disabled, pressuring businesses and public places to provide better wheelchair access. He spoke out on behalf of charities that raised money for medical research, especially those that dealt with ALS and similar conditions. He also was vocal on political issues, warning about the dangers of climate change, nuclear war, and more. He endorsed candidates that promised to address these problems and criticized those who did not.

In 2007 Hawking tried a new type of writing. He and his daughter, Lucy, coauthored a children's book, *George's Secret Key to the Universe.* The fictional book followed the adventures of a family and their supercomputer as they looked into the mysteries of the universe. Over the next decade, the writing duo followed up with four sequels. "Working with my father was a great thrill," Lucy Hawking said in an interview. "He has the amazing ability to hold enormous amounts of information in his head, but also to pick out relevant details and make brief comments, which can completely

PARTY OF NONE

In 2009 Hawking hosted a lavish party in Cambridge. Hawking sat alone in his wheelchair, waiting for his guests to show up. But nobody came. That's because Hawking didn't send out the invitations for the party until the next day. Hawking invited all time travelers from the future to his dinner party. He explained that if time travel were possible, somebody should have attended. Because nobody came, Hawking reasoned, travel backward in time must not be possible.

transform your way of thinking. . . . He was an absolute pleasure to work with and I felt very honored to have this opportunity."

In 2014 Working Title Films released a biopic on Hawking, his life, and his marriage. The film, *The Theory of Everything*, starred Eddie Redmayne as Hawking. It was well received by critics and was nominated for five Academy Awards, including Best Picture. Redmayne won the 2014 Academy Award for Best Performance by an Actor in a Leading Role.

In his later years, Hawking became more concerned

Eddie Redmayne (*left*) and Stephen Hawking pose on the red carpet after Redmayne won a British Academy Film Award for his performance in *The Theory of Everything*.

about the human race's long-term survival. Among the threats that worried him were war, climate change, and the rise of intelligent machines. "With climate change, overdue asteroid strikes, epidemics, and population growth, our own planet is increasingly precarious," Hawking explained in 2017. He predicted that if humans didn't change their ways, the human race would likely be extinct within one thousand years. Later, he changed that figure, declaring that the species could be in danger in as little as one hundred years.

Hawking argued that colonizing outer space was the key to humanity's survival. "Although the chance of a disaster to planet Earth in a given year may be quite low, it adds up over time, and becomes a near certainty in the next thousand or ten thousand years," Hawking said. "By that time we should have spread out into space, and to other stars, so a disaster on Earth would not mean the end of the human race."

Death and Legacy

By 2018 Hawking had survived more than half a century with ALS. Living so long with the disease is almost unheard of. Only 5 percent of people with ALS live longer than twenty years. But that year, his health declined sharply. On March 14, 2018, Hawking passed away. According to his family, the legendary physicist died peacefully. He was seventy-six years old.

Hawking's funeral was held on March 31 at Great St Mary's Church in Cambridge. His body was cremated, and his ashes were placed near the graves of famous scientists Sir Isaac Newton and Charles Darwin.

Hawking was a giant in the field of physics. His work to unravel the mysteries of black holes, the origin of the universe, and the physics of the quantum world made him one of the greatest thinkers of the century. His ability to communicate his love of science to the masses made him an icon. That he achieved all he did while battling a fatal disease made him even more remarkable.

Jane Hawking (*center*), Timothy Hawking (*second from right*), and Lucy Hawking (*right*) attend Stephen Hawking's funeral on March 31, 2018. Also in attendance were many celebrities, including Eddie Redmayne.

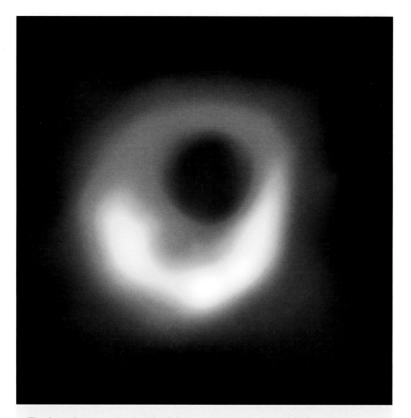

The first photograph of a black hole, revealed in April 2019, shows a gravitationally warped view of the event horizon.

"Those who knew Hawking would clearly appreciate the dominating presence of a real human being, with an enormous zest for life, great humor, and tremendous determination, yet with normal human weaknesses, as well as his more obvious strengths," wrote his friend and fellow physicist Roger Penrose in Hawking's obituary. "It seems clear that he took great delight in his commonly perceived role as 'the No. 1 celebrity scientist'; huge audiences would attend his public lectures, perhaps not always just for scientific [reasons]."

IMPORTANT DATES

1942   Hawking is born on January 8 in Oxford, England.

1950   The Hawking family moves to St Albans.

1959   Hawking enrolls at University College in Oxford.

1962   Hawking begins his graduate studies at the University of Cambridge.

1962   Hawking begins to notice changes in his strength and coordination.

1963   Hawking is diagnosed with ALS. His doctors tell him he has only two years to live.

1965   Hawking marries Jane Wilde.

1966   Hawking completes his doctorate at Cambridge.

1974   Hawking presents his theory that black holes are not eternal and slowly evaporate over time.

1979   Hawking is appointed Lucasian Professor of Mathematics at Cambridge.

1985   Hawking survives a brush with death as a result of pneumonia. The illness robs him of his ability to speak.

1988   Hawking publishes the best seller, *A Brief History of Time*.

1993   Hawking makes his first television appearance, as himself, in *Star Trek: The Next Generation*.

1997   Hawking appears on the six-part television series *Stephen Hawking's Universe*.

2001   Hawking publishes *The Universe in a Nutshell*.

2014   *The Theory of Everything*, a biopic about Hawking's life, is released.

2018   Hawking dies on March 14.

SOURCE NOTES

12 Stephen Hawking, *My Brief History* (New York: Bantam Books, 2013), 24.

14 Kitty Ferguson, *Stephen Hawking: An Unfettered Mind* (New York: Palgrave Macmillan, 2012), 29.

15 Ferguson.

18 "An Exceptional Man," *BMJ* 324, no. 7325 (June 22, 2002): 1478, https://www.ncbi.nlm.nih.gov/pmc/articles/PMC1123440/.

18–19 "An Exceptional Man."

29–30 "Stephen Hawking Tells How Doctors Offered to Turn Off Life Support in 1985," *Guardian* (US edition), July 28, 2013, https://www.theguardian.com/science/2013/jul/28/stephen-hawking-doctors-life-support/.

31 "Editor's Choice 1988," *New York Times*, December 4, 1988, http://movies2.nytimes.com/books/98/12/06/specials/editorschoice88.html.

37–38 "Q & A: Stephen Hawking and Daughter Lucy," *Today*, November 1, 2007, https://www.today.com/popculture/q-stephen-hawking-daughter-lucy-wbna21550559/.

39 Arjun Kharpal, "Stephen Hawking Says Humans Must Colonize Another Planet in 100 Years or Face Extinction," CNBC, May 5, 2017, https://www.cnbc.com/2017/05/05/stephen-hawking-human-extinction-colonize-planet.html.

39 Kharpal.

41 Roger Penrose, "'Mind Over Matter': Stephen Hawking—Obituary by Roger Penrose," *Guardian* (US edition), March 14, 2018, https://www.theguardian.com/science/2018/mar/14/stephen-hawking-obituary/.

SELECTED BIBLIOGRAPHY

Ferguson, Kitty. *Stephen Hawking: An Unfettered Mind*. New York: Palgrave Macmillan, 2012.

Hawking, Stephen. *A Brief History of Time*. New York: Bantam Books, 1998.

——. *My Brief History*. New York: Bantam Books, 2013.

"Stephen Hawking Tells How Doctors Offered to Turn Off Life Support in 1985." *Guardian* (US edition), July 28, 2013. https://www.theguardian.com/science/2013/jul/28/stephen-hawking-doctors-life-support/.

Stephen Hawking: The Official Website. Accessed January 4, 2020. http://www.hawking.org.uk/.

White, Michael, and John Gribbin. *Stephen Hawking: A Life in Science*. Washington, DC: Joseph Henry, 2002.

FURTHER READING

BOOKS

Doeden, Matt. *Albert Einstein: Relativity Rock Star.* Minneapolis: Lerner
    Publications, 2020.
    Who was Albert Einstein? How did he change the way people
    thought about the universe? Learn more in this biography of
    history's greatest physicist.

Gaughan, Richard. *Physics in Your Everyday Life.* New York: Enslow,
    2020.
    What is physics? What role does it play in daily life? Learn more
    about light, electricity, states of matter, and more in this book.

Gigliotti, Jim. *Who Was Stephen Hawking?* New York: Penguin
    Workshop, 2019.
    Learn more about Hawking, his career, life, and battle with ALS.

WEBSITES

Ducksters: Stephen Hawking
https://www.ducksters.com/biography/scientists/stephen_hawking.php
Check out this brief biography of Hawking, including his major life events and achievements.

Kids Discover
https://online.kidsdiscover.com
Explore topics on a wide range of science news and breakthroughs, including the latest in physics.

National Geographic Kids: Black Holes
https://kids.nationalgeographic.com/explore/space/black-holes/
What are black holes? How do they form? And how do scientists find them? Read more about these fascinating objects in this easy-to-read article.

INDEX